W9-DGI-710

WITHDRAWN

Clergy

Career Assessments & Their Meaning
Childcare Worker
Clergy
Computer Programmer
Financial Advisor
Firefighter
Homeland Security Officer
Journalist
Manager
Military & Elite Forces Officer
Nurse
Politician
Professional Athlete & Sports Official
Psychologist
Research Scientist
Social Worker
Special Education Teacher
Veterinarian

CAREERS WITH CHARACTER

Clergy

Kenneth McIntosh

Mason Crest

Mason Crest
450 Parkway Drive, Suite D
Broomall, PA 19008
www.masoncrest.com

Printed in the Hashemite Kingdom of Jordan.

First printing
9 8 7 6 5 4 3 2 1

Series ISBN: 978-1-4222-2750-3
ISBN: 978-1-4222-2753-4
ebook ISBN: 978-1-4222-9049-1

The Library of Congress has cataloged the
        hardcopy format(s) as follows:

Library of Congress Cataloging-in-Publication Data

McIntosh, Kenneth, 1959-
  Clergy / Kenneth McIntosh.
      pages cm. – (Careers with character)
  Audience: Grade 7 to 8.
  Includes index.
  ISBN 978-1-4222-2753-4 – ISBN 978-1-4222-2750-3 (series) – ISBN 978-1-4222-9049-1 (ebook)
  1. Clergy–Office–Juvenile literature. I. Title.
  BV660.3.M35 2014
  253'.2–dc22
                        2013007004

Produced by Vestal Creative Services.
www.vestalcreative.com

Photo Credits:
Comstock: pp. 13, 17, 23, 24, 26, 33, 40, 46
Corbis: pp. 10, 56, 57
Corel: pp. 50, 66
Monkey Business Images | Dreamstime.com: p. 38
Oleksandr Lysenko | Dreamstime.com: p. 16
Penn Clark: p. 58
PhotoAlto: pp. 27, 49, 51, 69, 79, 86, 87
PhotoDisc: pp. 12, 25, 30, 32, 41, 42, 43, 62, 64, 72, 74, 75, 82, 84, 85
Sergey Rogovets | Dreamstime.com: p. 54
Viola Ruelke Gommer: pp. 65, 77, 78, 89

To the best knowledge of the publisher, all other images are in the public domain. If any image has been inadvertantly uncredited or miscredited, please notify Vestal Creative Services, Vestal, New York 13850, so that rectification can be made for future printings.

CONTENTS

We each leave a fingerprint on the world.
Our careers are the work we do in life.
Our characters are shaped by the choices
we make to do good.
When we combine careers with character,
we touch the world with power.

INTRODUCTION

by Dr. Cheryl Gholar
and Dr. Ernestine G. Riggs

In today's world, the awesome task of choosing or staying in a career has become more involved than one would ever have imagined in past decades. Whether the job market is robust or the demand for workers is sluggish, the need for top-performing employees with good character remains a priority on most employers' lists of "must have" or "must keep." When critical decisions are being made regarding a company or organization's growth or future, job performance and work ethic are often the determining factors as to who will remain employed and who will not.

How does one achieve success in one's career and in life? Victor Frankl, the Austrian psychologist, summarized the concept of success in the preface to his book *Man's Search for Meaning* as: "The unintended side-effect of one's personal dedication to a course greater than oneself." Achieving value by responding to life and careers from higher levels of knowing and being is a specific goal of teaching and learning in "Careers with Character." What constitutes success for us as individuals can be found deep within our belief system. Seeking, preparing, and attaining an excellent career that aligns with our personality is an outstanding goal. However, an excellent career augmented by exemplary character is a visible expression of the human need to bring meaning, purpose, and value to our work.

Career education informs us of employment opportunities, occupational outlooks, earnings, and preparation needed to perform certain tasks. Character education provides insight into how a person of good character might choose to respond, initiate an action, or perform specific tasks in the presence of an ethical dilemma. "Careers with Character" combines the two and teaches students that careers are more than just jobs. Career development is incomplete without character development. What better way to explore careers and character than to make them a single package to be opened, examined, and reflected upon as a means of understanding the greater whole of who we are and what work can mean when one chooses to become an employee of character?

Character can be defined simply as "who you are even when no one else is around." Your character is revealed by your choices and actions. These bear your personal signature, validating the story of who you are. They are the fingerprints you leave behind on the people you meet and know; they are the ideas you bring into reality. Your choices tell the world what you truly believe.

Character, when viewed as a standard of excellence, reminds us to ask ourselves when choosing a career: "Why this particular career, for what purpose, and to what end?" The authors of "Careers with Character" knowledgeably and passionately, through their various vignettes, enable one to experience an inner journey that is both intellectual and moral. Students will find themselves, when confronting decisions in real life, more prepared, having had experiential learning opportunities through this series. The books, however, do not separate or negate the individual good from the academic skills or intellect needed to perform the required tasks that lead to productive career development and personal fulfillment.

Each book is replete with exemplary role models, practical strategies, instructional tools, and applications. In each volume, individuals of character work toward ethical leadership, learning how to respond appropriately to issues of not only right versus wrong, but issues of right versus right, understanding the possible benefits and consequences of their decisions. A wealth of examples is provided.

What is it about a career that moves our hearts and minds toward fulfilling a dream? It is our character. The truest approach to finding out who we are and what illuminates our lives is to look within. At the very heart of career development is good character. At the heart of good character is an individual who knows and loves the good, and seeks to share the good with others. By exploring careers and character together, we create internal and external environments that support and enhance each other, challenging students to lead conscious lives of personal quality and true richness every day.

Is there a difference between doing the right thing, and doing things right? Career questions ask, "What do you know about a specific career?" Character questions ask, "Now that you know about a specific career, what will you choose to do with what you know?" "How will you perform certain tasks and services for others, even when no one else is around?" "Will all individuals be given your best regardless of their socioeconomic background, physical condition, ethnicity, or religious beliefs?" Character questions often challenge the authenticity of what we say we believe and value in the workplace and in our personal lives.

Character and career questions together challenge us to pay attention to our lives and not fall asleep on the job. Career knowledge, self-knowledge, and ethical wisdom help us answer deeper questions about the meaning of work; they give us permission to transform our lives. Personal integrity is the price of admission.

The insight of one "ordinary" individual can make a difference in the world—if that one individual believes that character is an amazing gift to uncap knowledge and talents to empower the human community. Our world needs everyday heroes in the workplace—and "Careers with Character" challenges students to become those heroes.

The riots in Los Angeles after the Rodney King court case offered at least one member of the clergy an opportunity to display his character.

JOB REQUIREMENTS

Whatever career you choose, a good character will make you shine.

CHAPTER ONE

t was the worst week in the history of a great American city. On April 29, 1992, a jury found four white police officers not guilty in the beating of Rodney King, a black man. The riots that followed left 50 people dead and 4,000 injured. In the midst of the horror, one man put his life on the line for another man he didn't even know. At the intersection of Florence and Normandie Avenues, Pastor Bennie Newton, a 59-year-old African American, stood guard over Fidel Lopez, a Latino construction worker threatened by a mob. Fidel, an immigrant from Guatemala, had been pulled out of his truck and beaten on the head with a stereo speaker. Waving his Bible in his

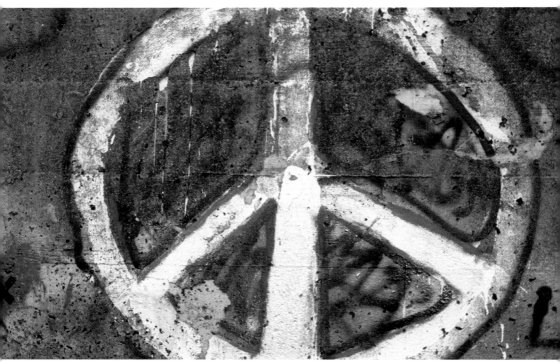

Members of the clergy work to spread peace—even in city streets where people may know very little external peace.

hand, Reverend Newton yelled at the attackers, "Kill him, and you have to kill me too!" After the riots, Pastor Newton gave more than $3,000 to help pay for Fidel Lopez's medical bills. Fidel later told people, "This good man saved my life."

Bennie Newton displayed remarkable courage and compassion in the midst of the violence, character traits that would have amazed people who knew him in his former life. He had served time in several tough prisons for a variety of crimes, including armed robbery, *pimping*, and drug possession. In the late 1970s, however, Newton changed the direction of his life. He attributed this to a spiritual awakening, and he then began the Light of Love Outreach Ministry, which helped young people, homeless people, and prisoners learn about God and improve themselves. He also

Many members of the clergy view their work as a call to spread God's blessing to the world.

began programs to help students in poor neighborhoods with their schoolwork. Someone who knew him said, "Saving lives was an everyday event for Bennie Newton." He was a man who cared deeply about other people, no matter what their race or background. He was also a professional clergyman.

Clergy are men and women who serve as spiritual leaders. They try to show people how God can make their lives better. They explain the sacred writings of their faiths. They prepare public worship services, teach religious education classes, and visit the sick. Clergy provide comfort and advice to people who struggle with family or personal problems. They lead ceremonies that mark the important transitions of life: birth, marriage, and death. In smaller churches or synagogues, clergy do secretarial work and administra-

Varieties of Judaism and Christianity

Orthodox Judaism
The smallest branch of Judaism, and the most conservative. They believe the Scriptures should be literally followed in every detail of life.

Conservative Judaism
A "middle of the road" approach. The Scripture (Torah) is studied carefully and applied with flexibility to modern concerns.

Reform Judaism
Most North American Jews today are Reform. They are the most flexible group in their understanding of Scriptures. They believe individuals should choose for themselves how to practice their faith.

Catholicism
The largest branch of Christianity with over a billion adherents. The Pope is recognized as spokesperson for the church. A central focus is on the sacraments, concrete and physical rituals that convey unseen and spiritual reality.

Orthodoxy
Separated from Roman Catholicism a thousand year ago, over refusal of the Pope's authority. Worship focuses on the Eucharist, and relies on images (icons) to help experience God. Orthodoxy follows beliefs and worship practices dating back to the early Christian church.

Pentacostalism
The fastest growing branch of Christianity, and the major Christian denomination in many developing nations. Worship focuses on direct experience of God's Spirit. Services are emotional and lively.

Evangelicalism
Very influential in North America today. Many Pentecostals and Mainline Protestants would also consider themselves Evangelicals. Emphasis is on the Bible as God's perfect written word to humankind. Worship emphasizes preaching of the Bible.

Mainline Protestantism
Denominations that split from Catholicism at the time of the Reformation in the 16th century or which grew out of those groups. These include: Episcopal, Congregational, Methodist, Lutheran, American Baptist, United Church of Christ, and *Presbyterian* churches. These churches are declining in numbers worldwide. Their beliefs and practices vary greatly, and they have a flexible approach to the Bible and moral issues.

tive work. Larger *Protestant* churches may hire a youth pastor who works with teenagers, a worship pastor who prepares services, an administrative pastor who directs daily operations, as well as a senior pastor who leads the team. There may also be pastors of small group ministries, pastors for senior citizens, for family needs, or for children.

Some members of the clergy do not serve a church or synagogue. They may serve as chaplains who provide spiritual care to the armed forces, prisons, hospitals, or corporations. Some work in missions or social service agencies serving the poor. Others teach in schools. There are clergy who live in monasteries, devoting their lives to prayer and meditation. Vacation cruise boats hire chaplains, and clergy serve in national parks. There are even Catholic nuns who minister in a traveling circus.

Members of the clergy view their work as much more than just a job. For most professions, people begin by asking: "What do I enjoy doing? What kind of pay will I earn? What kind of education will be

Members of the clergy study the scriptures of their faith.

Looking Good or Being Good?

Stephen Covey, in *Seven Habits of Highly Effective People*, suggests society has shifted from a "character ethic," which says success comes from good moral choices, to "personality ethic," which is concerned with image or appearance. He believes personality ethic is to blame for many problems in our world today. All the great religions emphasize the importance of good character over good appearance.

required?" For members of the clergy, however, there is another more important question: "Is God calling me to be a spiritual leader?"

The "call" may come in many different forms. The most famous preacher of the 20th century, Billy Graham, describes his call this way: "I just kept sensing that God was calling me. One night I was out on the 18th green of the Temple Terrace Golf

Course, and it was a moonlit night. I sat out there and I could just sense that God was speaking to me and He wanted me to work for Him. And I said to the Lord that night, 'I'll go where you want me to go, I'll be what you want me to be.'" While clergy in a variety of traditions differ as to the exact form of the call experience, they all agree God chooses those who will serve him as spiritual leaders. Yet the "call" alone is not sufficient preparation for ministry.

Most faiths require years of education for their spiritual leaders. Three out of four clergy have at least a bachelor's degree (four-year degree) in college. Protestant Christian churches require at least a four-year degree from a *Bible college*, some require a three-year master's degree in theology following college. Sixty-three percent of Protestant pastors hold a master's degree, and Roman Catholic

Clergy have the chance to participate in life's important moments—like weddings.

18

A Call to Ministry That Changed History

At age 12, Agnes Bojaxhiu sensed God calling her to serve him, but she wondered how she could know for certain. She asked her priest, "How can I be sure?" He answered, "Through your joy. If you feel really happy by the idea that God might call you to serve him, then this is the evidence that you have a call. The deep inner joy that you feel is the compass that indicates your direction in life." She followed that sense of joy, and later became known to the world as Mother Teresa of Calcutta.

priests tend to be even more highly educated. Four years of theology study after their bachelor's degree are required before entering the priesthood. Rabbis must take four or five years of study beyond a bachelor's degree. In addition to theology, Jewish spiritual leaders are trained in a variety of forms of public service. In Islam, clerics often begin their theological studies by memorizing the entire Koran, word for word. After that, they go on to study its meaning.

As you can see, clergy of all kinds are expected to be well schooled. Yet even the call to ministry and extensive schooling are not enough to prepare a woman or man for spiritual leadership.

Members of the clergy face unusually difficult conditions in their work. Ninety percent of clergy work more than 46 hours each week, and many work more than 60 hours. Clergy are called regularly to deal with crises such as marriage conflicts, severe illnesses, or the deaths of the people they serve. Most clergy are "on call" every day of the week. They receive phone calls for help late at night and during weekends. For these reasons, clergy have unusually high rates of depression and emotional exhaustion. Clergy are expected to respond to difficult situations with consistently virtuous behavior. They must be people of outstanding character.

Thomas Lickona, an expert in character education, says, "Good character consists of knowing the good, desiring the good, and doing the good—habits of the mind, habits of the heart, and habits of action." In following chapters, this book will display the character qualities required of spiritual leaders. These qualities include:

- Integrity and trustworthiness
- Respect and compassion
- Justice and fairness
- Responsibility
- Courage
- Self-discipline and diligence
- Citizenship

Character makes people attractive from the inside out. In journalist Lucy Kaylin's book *For the Love of God*, about American nuns, she says she was used to interviewing movie stars and models who are "like Japanese lanterns: pretty, paper-thin, and empty inside." She realized the nuns she interviewed "were exactly the opposite . . . their exteriors are quite unremarkable. Their strength and inspiration all come from within, which I think is what makes a lot of nuns look as if there is something burning brightly within them."

Whatever career you eventually choose for yourself, when you decide to be a person of character, you too will be lit from the inside out.

Character is not in the mind. It is in the will.

—Fulton John Sheen, North American archbishop

Sexuality is a difficult issue to handle with integrity and trustworthiness.

INTEGRITY AND TRUSTWORTHINESS

No matter how much we may have messed up in the past, a life of integrity is still an option for the future.

CHAPTER TWO

"**I** have experienced the heights and depths of sin and forgiveness, I ask you now to forgive me and restore me to ministry." These were the words Pete told the committee who held his future in their hands. His story is told in *The Hidden World of the Pastor*, by Kenneth Swetland.

Pete's career as a clergyman had gone very differently from the way he intended. While Pete was a young man serving in the army, he and his wife Barbara experienced a new relationship with God. Three years later, he felt strongly called to ministry and began taking courses at a *seminary*. He and Barbara often quarreled, but he enjoyed his studies. After graduation, he began work as a Presbyterian pastor. His congregation grew and he was successful. At the same time, however, he and his family became more and more distant from each other. While these things were going on, he began counseling a married woman at the church named Janie.

As Pete's marriage grew worse, he found himself seeing Janie more and more. He knew he was romantically attracted to her, knew this was wrong, yet felt powerless to stop. Before long they were meeting secretly and having sex. Pete felt horribly guilty. He had preached sermons against adultery. How could he be a pastor and break God's rules like this? He decided to tell one of the important officials in his church about the affair. He also offered to resign as pastor.

That Sunday, the congregation had a meeting. They accepted his resignation. They also decided to give Pete's salary to Barbara for the next six months. Barbara decided to divorce Pete and made him move out of their house. He was forced to live at the YMCA and scramble for odd jobs. His own children refused to see him, and former church members would avoid him or express their anger when they saw him. He sank into deep depression and even thought about killing himself. Janie, in the meantime, had been divorced by her husband. She found Pete living in despair and took him into her apartment.

Some Definitions

The word integrity comes from the word integer, meaning "one" or wholeness. Persons with integrity will behave consistently wherever they are. In the synagogue and at home, with their family or with strangers, they are the same. They value the truth. For clergy, integrity requires a reasonable effort to live by the Holy Books and traditions of their faith. Trustworthiness is a virtue closely connected to integrity. Trustworthiness means we live up to the things that others expect from us.

For a long time Pete was afraid to go to church. He felt deeply ashamed. One day he forced himself to go to a church and speak with the pastor. He told his whole story and hid nothing. The pastor said, "I believe God's forgiveness is real. If you're sorry for what you've done, then seek God's forgiveness and he'll forgive you." For the first time in a long time, Pete felt God loved him.

Pete and Janie married. He found a good job and became active in their new church. As time went by, he began to help the pastor. People discovered his talents for church work, and he found renewed happiness serving God. Finally, the day came when he asked to become a minister again. A committee studied the story of his life. He had broken the promises he made as a pastor, promises made to God, to his wife, and to the church. But he was truly sorry.

A clergyperson who struggles with character issues can feel very lonely.

Should he be allowed to serve a congregation as pastor again? Would you respect a spiritual leader who has failed morally but asks to be forgiven?

Choices like this are, unfortunately, common. There is an old saying, "If you can't trust a pastor who can you trust?" Rabbis, pastors, and other clergy are assumed to be examples of integrity and trustworthiness, but they often fail. Clergy may use money that belongs to their congregation in illegal or inappropriate ways. At the very worst, clergy can abuse children or other vulnerable people under their care. When clergy fail to live with integrity, people around them suffer.

Failures of integrity do not usually come in one big step. For instance, Pastor Owen Jones did not normally see young women for counseling during hours when they would be alone. He made an exception to his own rule with Susan, a college girl at his church. She sounded very upset but couldn't take time off from classes during the day, so he agreed to meet her late Wednesday night. In his office, the attractive young woman sat on the couch and cried while he sat behind his desk. He felt she might interpret his body

If a pastor aligns his life with scripture, he will treat others with integrity.

Faced with an ethical dilemma, each individual—whether a member of the clergy or a great "saint" of the faith—must determine for himself what is right.

language as being cold and distant, and he decided to move closer. She slid into his arms for comfort. Again not wishing to seem distant, he allowed her to hug him. Then he realized her hug seemed more than sisterly.

Pastor Jones had fallen prey to self-deception. He knew it was inappropriate to be alone in the building with a young woman, and he knew clergy and counselors must keep a professional distance from people they try to help. He had allowed his feelings to defeat common sense, breaking one rule after another. His mind raced

How Do I Know Right from Wrong in a Situation?

The Josephson Institute has identified these two "ethics guides" that can help anyone to live with integrity:

- The Golden Rule. Are you treating others as you would want to be treated?
- Publicity. Would you be comfortable if your actions were to be publicized? How would you feel seeing it on the front page of tomorrow's papers?

Spiritual leaders who live their lives with integrity shine like lights for the rest of the world to follow.

Warning! Warning!

The Josephson Institute of Ethics has identified four enemies of integrity. These are:

- Self-interest—the things we want.
- Self-protection—the things we want to avoid.
- Self-deception—a refusal to see what is really happening.
- Self-righteousness—an attitude that says we should not have to live by the same standards as other people.

frantically. How could he get out of this situation without making things worse? Once he was out of the situation, should he admit to anyone else what had almost happened? He dearly wished he had not gotten into this mess in the first place. Faced with an ethical dilemma, he must choose whether he will behave with integrity and trustworthiness. It was not too late for him to choose a moral course of action. He could pull back from Susan and retreat once more behind his desk.

While many clergy have failed morally, many other spiritual leaders have inspired others with their integrity and trustworthiness. Several years ago, I sat beside my family inside a little church located within one of the worst areas of a large city. The church was filled for the funeral service of my wife's uncle, Jack Blaes. Uncle Jack spent his adult life as a clergyman. He served several churches. Some were little country churches, and then there was this church in the inner city. None of his congregations had wealthy people. They did not pay him much, though he worked hard.

His daughter stood and had this to say about her father: "He was always there to listen—and to understand—he lived like he taught." That's what a good clergyperson does. They walk the talk.

Do you?

You've got to get the mind cleared out before you put the truth in it.

—Louis Farrakhan, Nation of Islam leader

Some nuns serve God by hiding themselves away from the world to pray—while others serve God by immersing themselves in some of the world's darkest places.

RESPECT AND COMPASSION

Acts of love may not be easy—but they have the power to change the world.

CHAPTER THREE

"**S**ister Nancy doesn't look or sound like the stereotypical nun." As Lucy Kaylin describes Sister Nancy in her book, *For the Love of God*, the nun wears jeans and flannel shirts, sometimes with a pack of cigarettes sticking out of her pocket. Her words can be blunt and earthy. No one messes with her, which is good, because she deals with some pretty tough customers. Sister Nancy works with other nuns at the Dwelling Place, a shelter for homeless women near New York's Port Authority Bus Terminal.

Twenty years ago, a group of nuns raised funds to buy a four-story apartment building in this grimy part of the *Big Apple*. Since then, the Dwelling Place has provided dinners for as many as two

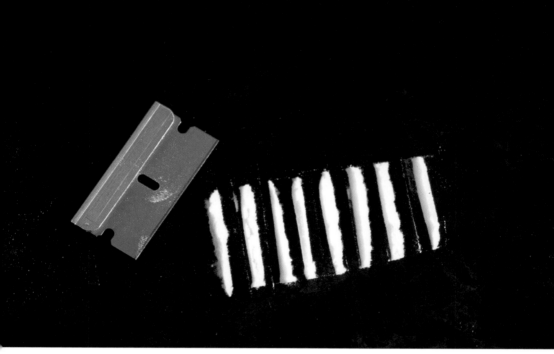

Drugs are a reality in almost any congregation, particularly when the congregation is made up of homeless people.

hundred women at a time in a room built for 80. The nuns have been punched and even bitten by crack addicts in their facility. But the sisters' respect and compassion for others don't waver. They counsel homeless women, feed and hug them, help them find jobs and places to live, remind them to take medications, throw holiday parties for them, and assist them through pregnancies.

Lucy Kaylin says, "The Dwelling Place doesn't look like the holiest place in New York. But if holiness means living as Jesus did by loving and serving the poor, then the Dwelling Place is the Vatican of the

In place of "compassion and respect," you could use a four-letter word—love. When you value this character quality, you put yourself in others' places. You treat them the way you would like to be treated yourself.

Sayings on Compassion from Four Religions

Jewish
In the Torah, God says to Moses: "You shall not insult the deaf, or place a stumbling block before the blind . . . do not deal basely with your fellows. Do not profit by the blood of your neighbor. You shall not hate your kinsman . . . you shall not take vengeance or bear a grudge . . . love your neighbor as yourself."

Buddhist
The Buddha said, ". . . Whatever living beings there be: feeble or strong, tall, stout or medium, short, small or large, without exception, may all beings be happy! Let none deceive another, not despise any person whatsoever in any place. Let him not wish any harm to another out of anger or ill-will. Just as a mother would protect her only child at the risk of her own life, even so, let him cultivate a boundless heart toward all beings."

Christian
Jesus, in his most famous sermon, said: "You have heard that it was said, 'You shall love your neighbor and hate your enemy.' But I say to you, Love your enemies and pray for those who persecute you, so that you may be children of your Father in heaven; for he makes his sun rise on the evil and on the good, and sends rain on the righteous and on the unrighteous."

Muslim
Mohammad taught his followers, "Feed the hungry and visit the sick, and free the captive if he be unjustly confined. Assist any person oppressed, whether Muslim or non-Muslim."

If you were the spiritual leader of a large urban church, how would you demonstrate respect and compassion to the drug users you encountered?

street." The actions of Sister Nancy and her coworkers at the Dwelling Place consistently demonstrate the virtues of respect and compassion.

Respect and compassion are among the most important principles taught in all the world's great religions. Yet identifying the most compassionate response in a situation is not always easy. Imagine yourself in the following situation.

You are the spiritual leader for a small urban congregation. A portion of your church's funds are regularly set aside for charitable giving to persons in the neighborhood. Every week, people call asking for help to buy groceries, provide diapers for their infants, pay heating bills, and so on. You know you do not have enough money

Buddha taught that humans should have a "boundless heart toward all beings."

to meet everyone's needs, but you do your best to help as many as you can.

One day, a man named Bob stops in at your office. He is soft spoken and polite. He explains his son is ill and needs medicine. Welfare helps with part of the cost, but he must provide a small co-payment. His money is gone, and his child needs medicine. He shows you a doctor's prescription for the child's medication. You are impressed with Bob's apparent sincerity, and you decide to give him a large portion of the congregation's charitable funds so he can buy the medicine for the child.

The next day, you see Bob again. He doesn't see you . . . because he is completely stoned, lying on the sidewalk with several other men you recognize as drug addicts. Several weeks later, Bob comes in again, asking once again for help with his son's medicine.

Should you help him? It appears he is a drug addict. At the same time, he may have a child who really needs the medicine. You don't have enough money for all the people who ask,

R-E-S-P-E-C-T

As explained by the Josephson Institute of Ethics, "The way one shows respect varies," but all respect has this in common:

- It treats people as if they are valuable.
- It includes oneself.
- We are morally obligated to treat everyone with respect, regardless of who they are and what they have done.
- We have a responsibility to be the best we can be in all situations, even when dealing with unpleasant people.
- Respect focuses on the worth and dignity of the individual.
- Respect prohibits violence, humiliation, manipulation, and exploitation.
- It reflects notions such courtesy, dignity, tolerance, and acceptance.

When we practice respect and compassion for all, we become lights that shine for the world to see.

so should you help someone like Bob when you know he is likely to misuse the money?

Rushworth Kidder, in his book *How Good People Make Tough Choices* suggests three ways to approach a difficult moral choice:

- Ends-based thinking: Do whatever produces the greatest good for the greatest number.
- Rule-based thinking: If everyone in the world followed the rule of action I am following, would that create the greatest good?
- Care-based thinking: Do to others what you would like them to do for you.

If you follow ends-based thinking, you might decide not to help Bob, because other people need help also. Considering how many other people deserve help, it makes sense not to give to those you know are likely to misuse the funds you give them. If you follow rule-based thinking, you are also likely not to give. If everyone stopped giving money to people who abuse drugs, they might be more likely to seek help for their addictions. But what about care-based thinking? If you were a person with an addiction, would you want people to give you money or not? If you have a sick child, does that change your answer? If people demonstrate trust in you, even if you are unworthy of their trust, is that likely to make you a better person? Would you help Bob?

Clergy must carefully consider how best to show respect and compassion for the people they serve. They need to consider principles for ethical decision-making, like those listed above. They study the Holy Writings and traditions of their faith. Yet clergy also believe they have a greater resource to draw upon when making tough choices. Prayer and meditation guide many of the decisions made by spiritual leaders. The form of their prayers may vary greatly, but Muslim imams, Protestant pastors, Jewish rabbis, and Catholic priests and nuns all agree that communication with God provides a sense of peace and "rightness" for difficult situations.

Mother Teresa, famous for her life of compassion, wrote: "Without prayer I could not work for even half an hour. I get my strength from God through prayer. It sustains, helps, and gives us all the joy to carry out what we need to do. . . . Every act of love is a prayer."

You may or may not choose to one day become a member of the clergy. But acts of love can be a part of your life today.

Love stretches your heart and makes you big inside.
—Margaret Walker

Not all congregations sit in pews dressed in their Sunday best!

JUSTICE AND FAIRNESS

Justice is an important character quality—but sometimes mercy is equally important. . . .

CHAPTER FOUR

The gang kids in East L.A. call him G-Dog, or simply "G." His real name is Greg Boyle. He is a *Jesuit* priest who has become famous for his work among the Latino street gangs. He serves as pastor at Dolores Mission church, the poorest Catholic *parish* in Los Angeles. It also has the dubious distinction of being located amid the highest level of gang violence in America. Within a few miles of the church are eight separate armies of adolescents, with names like the Clarence Street Locos, the East L.A. Dukes, the Mob Crew, and Al Capone. These gangs are armed with deadly firearms and separated by mutual hatred.

Father Greg has done what few ministers could or would do: he has become pastor, father figure, and best friend to the boys in

Justice and Mercy in the Holy Books

The Hebrew Bible
The Prophet Micah said: "He has showed you, mortals, what is good. And what does the Lord require of you? To act justly, and to love mercy."

The Christian Scriptures
The Apostle James said, "Speak and act as those who are going to be judged by the law that gives freedom . . . mercy triumphs over judgment!"

The Muslim Koran
The Koran begins, "Praise be to Allah. Most gracious. Most merciful. Master of the Day of Judgment."

The Muslim scriptures, the Koran, teach both justice and mercy.

If you were a clergyperson working with gang members, what would you do if you knew one of them was carrying a gun? How would you demonstrate justice and fairness?

the gangs. He helps them find jobs, gets them new clothes to work in, provides temporary housing, loves them, and prays with them. When tragedy strikes (and it strikes often), he presides at their funerals.

Father Greg is committed to never giving up hope for the homeboys. He has been criticized for extending unconditional love to violent young men whom others regard as beyond reform. He defends his commitment to them, saying, "God never gives up on us." This is not necessarily an easy thing for Father Greg to do, however. Working constantly with young criminals, Father Greg has to make wise and difficult choices, especially regarding justice and fairness. His unique ministry often draws him into gray areas where the police and the law are concerned.

One difficult situation involved a young man named Gustavo Vía Real, better known on the street as "Happy." Happy was picked up by the police for possessing a handgun. According to Happy, the police beat him while he was in custody. He was taken to a hospital, and en route to the X-ray room, Happy escaped. He fled through enemy gang neighborhoods, running as fast as he could, wearing only a hospital gown.

According to Father Greg, the police attempted to pressure the gang kids to turn in Happy. It is claimed the police beat up members of Happy's gang and threatened to do so until he was found. Meanwhile, the police claimed Father Greg was hiding Happy at Dolores Mission. Father Greg wasn't, but he *was* seeing Happy. Happy would call or visit the priest almost every day while he was on the run from the law.

Is justice the same as revenge? Or are justice and mercy somehow related?

Christ preached mercy as well as justice.

What would you do in Father Greg's position? As a person of character, you must do what is fair. So you must ask yourself, "Fair to whom?" If you think in terms of the law, then the fairest thing would be to turn in the young man. What would be fairest for his fellow gang members? They are getting beat up, yet they would rather be mistreated than rat on a friend. Would it be right to betray their trust in this matter? What is fair for Happy? He broke the law, but he also claims he was himself a victim. Where do victims of the police go for justice? Finally, it would be unfair for Father Greg to violate the sacred traditions of his faith. Confessions made to a priest are confidential, and clergy are expected to keep such confidences utterly, absolutely, and without regard to circumstances. Taking all these factors into account, what would be the right thing to do?

In considering the situation, Father Greg not only had to consider the issue of fairness; he also had to balance justice against mercy. Justice and fairness require that all people be given the same liberties, rights, and rules. If one person breaks a rule, he or she should be punished exactly like the next person who breaks that rule. If someone breaks the rule and is not punished, then jus-

The Christian New Testament provides this example of mercy overriding the demands of justice:

As [Jesus] was speaking, the teachers of the religious law ... brought a woman they had caught in the act of adultery. They put her in front of the crowd.

"Teacher," they said to Jesus, "this woman was caught in the very act of adultery. The law of Moses says to stone her. What do you say?"

...They kept demanding an answer, so [Jesus] stood up ... and said, "All right, stone her. But let those who have never sinned throw the first stone." ...

When the accusers heard this, they slipped away one by one, beginning with the oldest, until only Jesus was left in the middle of the crowd with the woman. Then Jesus ... said to her, "Where are your accusers? Didn't even one of them condemn you?"

"No, Lord," she said.

And Jesus said, "Neither do I." (John 8:3-5, 7, 9-11, New Living Translation)

tice has not been done. Mercy, however, goes beyond the letter of the law. Mercy considers that sometimes more good is done when people do not receive their deserved punishment.

Rushworth Kidder, an authority on ethics, writes: "The claims of justice urge us to stick by our principles, hold to the rules despite the pressures of the moment, pursue fairness without attention to personalities or situations." That's why statues and paintings of Lady Justice always show her blindfolded . . . so she will play no favorites. "Mercy, by contrast, is never blind," Kidder continues. "Mercy impels us to love without condition or restriction—beyond all laws, and sometimes in violation of them." Considering what to do with Happy, Father Greg not only has to think about what is just or fair for the community. As a priest, he is committed personally to the best for Happy. As a servant of God, he believes he must demonstrate God's unconditional mercy.

Clergy must know when to be guided by their sense of fairness . . . and when to be guided by mercy. They must be careful not to play favorites. If there is a disagreement, the person who gives great amounts of money to the congregation must be treated equally with the person who gives little. A longtime member of the synagogue should get equal consideration as the newcomer. The woman who is the head of a corporation must be treated with the same rights and privileges as the person who lives off welfare. Like Lady Justice, Christian ministers, Jewish rabbis, and Muslim imams must be blind to the differences between people.

And yet one of the chief roles of this profession is to act like a signpost that points people toward life's deeper spiritual meaning. As a result, sometimes clergy must look beyond rules and demonstrate the undeserved mercy of God. When someone takes money out of the offering, it may be far better to speak compassionately rather than call the police. If a church member falls into moral sin, a wise clergyperson will overlook the failure rather than threaten disgrace.

In your life, do you balance justice and mercy?

Love and justice march together. . . . You can't have one without the other.

—Stanley Booth-Clibborn, Anglican bishop

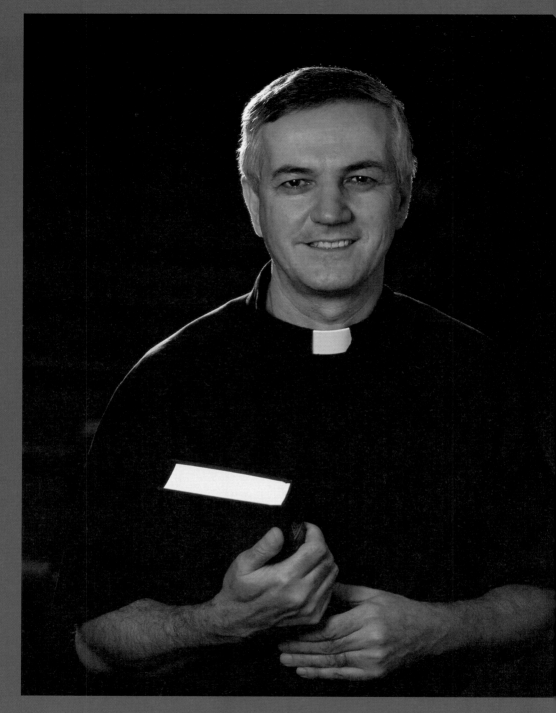

A good pastor is serious about his responsibility to his congregation.

RESPONSIBILITY

*True responsibility means we don't take on
more commitments than we can handle.*

CHAPTER FIVE

Stefan Ulfstein's book *Pastors Off the Record* tells dozens of true stories of anonymous pastors. One of these is a young man who pastors a church in Tijuana, Mexico, just south of the California-U.S. border. He "looks like the stereotypical Southern California beach bum." Yet he displays a great sense of responsibility for his little flock. As he tells the story, "I never wanted to be a pastor." He began working with the Mexican people as a *laypersons'* outreach ministry from his church in San Diego, but when a little church started up, it needed a pastor, and he realized no one else was likely to do the job. Like Father Greg's parish in the States, the Tijuana *barrio* is rife with drugs and violence. Attendance at the church service on Sunday ranges between 80 and 140 people, depending on the weather, violence, or political troubles.

When asked to give an example of a typical day in ministry, the pastor says: "Tomorrow I'm getting together with Mexican churchmen to dig a pit for an outhouse. We'll talk, and pray, and maybe eat together." When asked how he keeps going with hard work, little reward, and great challenges, he says: "It finally comes down to understanding that you're not working with the whole world. I can only work with the people I'm with, one at a time." Though this pastor works hard, his labors are not without their reward. He says, "I feel a satisfaction. When I see a guy like Carlos, whose life has been such a wreck—drugs, abandonment, crime, prison—walking with the Lord, it's right. It's a privilege to serve." Successful clergy take seriously their responsibility to help the people they serve.

Are You a Responsible Person?

According to the Character Counts Foundation, people who value responsibility:

- Think before they act; they consider the possible consequences of their actions.
- Accept responsibility for the consequences of their choices.
- Don't blame others for their mistakes or take credit for others' achievements.
- Don't make excuses.
- Set a good example for others.
- Pursue excellence in all they do.
- Do the best with what they have.
- Are dependable: others can rely on them.

Most of what clergy do is one-on-one care: counseling people with private problems, visiting the sick, getting to know members in their homes. Clergy are also responsible to God. They spend hours in private prayer. Almost none of this work is "checked on" by other people. Though most clergy answer to a board, these boards usually

A member of the clergy is responsible for representing his faith wherever he is—in a house of worship or in the street going about his ordinary business.

If members of the clergy act as lighthouses for the rest of the world, are they responsible to meet the needs of everyone they encounter—or are they responsible for making sure their own light does not go out?

do not meet more than once a month. If clergy lacked responsibility, they could get by with little real effort. Yet, clergy work more hours in an average week than people in any other profession.

It isn't always easy to be responsible. When I graduated from seminary, the graduation speaker told this story as a reminder of how clergy must be responsible to their priorities. The story concerns a lighthouse keeper in ancient times. He was sent to a remote coastal village and told to always have a good amount of dry firewood ready to light atop the stone light tower. There were dangerous, hidden rocks in the ocean near the point. If ships were not warned, they might run aground and sink.

For weeks, the light keeper had little to do but watch the ocean. Then, one day, a homeless man stopped by. Could he have some firewood to warm himself against the cold night? The light keeper figured it wouldn't hurt to give a little wood. The homeless man was deeply grateful, and on other cold nights the light keeper continued to give him wood. A few days after meeting the homeless man, a widow and her two daughters knocked on the light keeper's door. They had no wood to cook their food, and she had no money to pay for men to cut wood for them. Could they also have some wood? Again, the light keeper relented. After that, a lame man came who could not cut his own wood, and so on it went. Before long, the light keeper was a hero to needy people who lived near the light tower.

Then something truly awful happened. A large wooden ship filled with passengers came near the rocks. The light keeper saw the enormous boat headed for the breakers and ran to light the fire to warn them. But he had given away too much wood. He had only a few sticks left, not enough for a fire. He watched in anguish

Rabbis are responsible for their families as well as their congregations.

as the boat plowed into the rocks, and men and women tumbled into the freezing waters. Many people drowned. When the authorities investigated the crash, it was decided the light keeper was at fault and he was arrested.

What do you think? Was it right for the light keeper to give the wood for the needy people who asked him? Should he have refused them? Clergypersons— and all people of character—must prioritize their responsibilities.

Clergy are constantly asked to do things. There are rarely enough hours in a week to do everything for everyone who asks. While some things are good to do, they are not necessarily the most important things. The rabbi must remember his own wife and children come ahead of the congregation. If an imam has promised to do something, he must be sure to do that even if competing requests for help should arise. Tasks that are unpleasant must not be avoided, even if more enjoyable opportunities are at hand.

In order to be a responsible person, one must be careful not to take on too many commitments. I learned this from the pastor of the church I attended while going to college. I loved to do things at the church, so I said "yes" to every opportunity for service. I said "yes" to leading the college midweek fellowship. I said "yes" to teaching a Bible study in my dormitory. I said "yes" to meeting with other students for Bible discussions. I said "yes" to helping rebuild a home for refugees. There were more things I said "yes" to . . . but you get the idea. Unfortunately, I was also taking a full load of college courses, and I somehow thought I could have a social life as well.

Before long, I was proving rather unreliable with all my commitments. I would fail to show up for a Bible study because my homework was overdue for a class the next day. I would call up people and say we couldn't meet because other commitments were scheduled for the same time. I realized I had a problem. As a person who wanted to be responsible, I needed to reevaluate my life. I needed to learn to say yes only when I could keep my promise.

What about you? Do you keep your commitments?

Action springs . . . from a readiness for responsibility.

—Dietrich Bonhoeffer, Lutheran theologian

In today's world, clergy often encounter violence of one sort or another.

COURAGE

Whether the situation is a matter of life and death—or far more ordinary and trivial—resisting pressure from those around us always takes courage.

CHAPTER SIX

The young pastor had just fallen into bed after a long, difficult day when the phone rang. He picked up the phone and an angry voice said in his ear, "Listen, nigger, we've taken all we want from you; before next week you'll be sorry you ever came to Montgomery."

Martin Luther King, Jr. hung up the phone and got out of bed. He went to the kitchen and poured a cup of coffee, then sat down to think. He believed in his cause—a boycott to end segregation on Montgomery, Alabama, buses. He was convinced of his ideals, as well. He was following both Jesus and Mahatma Gandhi on the road of nonviolent social change. But there were other things to think about. He had a beautiful wife whom he adored and a new baby

Martin Luther King, Jr. was a courageous spiritual leader.

daughter. Only a month before, he had been jailed and released. He knew these threats were serious. Some sick-minded white people really did intend to kill him.

He says in his *Autobiography*, "I got to the point that I couldn't take it any longer. I was weak." In despair, he prayed, "Lord, I'm down here trying to do what's right. I am here taking a stand for what I believe. But Lord, I must confess that I'm weak now, I'm losing my courage. Now, I am afraid. And I can't let the people see me like this because if they see me weak and losing my courage, they will begin to get weak. I am at the end of my powers. I have nothing left. I've come to the point where I can't face it alone."

> Courage means doing what you know is right—even if you're scared.
>
> Courage is not the absence of fear, but the conquest of it.
> —anonymous

Spiritual leaders do not always see their prayers answered. This time, however, Dr. King received an immediate and powerful reply. As he relates the story, "I heard the voice of Jesus say still to fight on. He promised never to leave me alone. At that moment, I felt the presence of the Divine as I had never experienced him before. Almost at once, my fears began to go. My uncertainty disappeared. I was ready to face anything."

His newfound courage was about to be tested in ways he could hardly have imagined. Three nights later, as he was speaking at First Baptist Church, he noticed that some sort of news was spreading through the audience. When he asked what was happening, his good friend, Dr. Ralph Abernathy, replied, "Your house has been bombed." With his recent spiritual experience still fresh in mind, Dr. King was able to respond with amazing calm.

He arrived at his home to find his wife and daughter unharmed. A crowd of concerned African Americans was gathering. Dr. King saw some of the men had brought guns. Armed white policemen

Martin Luther King, Jr. lived his daily life with courage, despite the threats against his life.

were also converging on the scene. Tension and violence were in the air. Martin stepped onto the porch in front of his damaged house and spoke to the crowd, "We believe in law and order. Don't get your weapons. He who lives by the sword will perish by the sword. Remember that is what God said. I want you to love our enemies and let them know you love them." There were shouts of "Amen!" from the crowd. A voice called out, "We're with you all the way, Reverend." People went to their homes and the night was again peaceful.

For the next twelve years, Dr. Martin Luther King, Jr. repeatedly faced hatred and threats. On a Saturday morning in 1958, he was signing copies of his recently published book in a Harlem department store when he felt something sharp in his chest; he had been

What...and leave the ministry?

Most members of the clergy will not face the violence Martin Luther King, Jr. encountered—but their lives will still demand courage, as this cartoon demonstrates.

Many spiritual leaders find courage through prayer.

stabbed. Later, the doctor told him if he had sneezed after the stabbing he would have died. Then in May of 1963, the motel where he was staying was bombed. Many of Dr. King's friends, relatives, and associates were victims of white hatred and violence.

On April 3, 1968, Martin delivered his final sermon at a Memphis church. He spoke about courage to help others in need. He concluded, "Every now and then I think about my own death. I ask myself, What is it that I would like said? I'd like somebody to mention that day that Martin Luther King, Jr. tried to give his life serving others." The next day, an assassin's bullet found its mark.

When we think about courage, we naturally re-

> One isn't necessarily born with courage, but one is born with potential. Without courage, we cannot practice any other virtue with consistency. We can't be kind, true, merciful, generous, or honest.
> —Maya Angelou, quoted in *USA Today*, March 1998

call people like Dr. King. We imagine courageous public speeches, marches, and danger. Yet courage is not just a character trait for larger-than-life heroes. Ordinary women and men display courage in countless daily situations. Courage is what Craven Williams has described as "a cornerstone of character." Courage is the ability to display the other traits we have described—integrity, respect, justice, and so on—in situations where we are pressured or tempted to give up those values.

Character expert Thomas Lickona writes, "Courage helps young people respect themselves by resisting peer pressure to do things that are harmful to their own welfare. Courage helps all of us respect the rights of others when we face pressure to join the crowd in perpetrating an injustice. Courage also helps us to take bold, positive actions on behalf of others."

Clergy are constantly in situations that require moral courage. They face constant temptations to abandon what they know is right. Think about what you might do, if you were in one of the situations below.

- You are an imam, a Muslim spiritual leader. You know the Koran commands women to wear a head covering around their hair in public. You believe that is Allah's way of guarding women's modesty. After the September 11 terrorist attacks, some Americans are enraged at Islamic people. A few of the women from your mosque ask you whether they must continue wearing their veils in public. They know some Muslims have been killed by hateful fellow citizens. Must they wear the veil, or would it please Allah to take a safer route and be less obvious in public?

- You are the rabbi in a big city synagogue. You support Israel, yet you understand Arabs have also suffered in the conflicts between Palestinians and Jews. You host monthly meetings to discuss Arab-Israeli peacemaking. Now, there is increasing warfare in the Holy Land. Several families in the synagogue have suffered the death of loved ones in Israel, at the hands of Palestinian suicide bombers. They are understandably angry. They spread a petition through the synagogue and present it to you. Half the people in your synagogue have signed a paper that insists you stop hosting the Jewish-Arab meetings. If you continue the meetings, some members say they will leave. You have been called by God to serve these people, yet you believe Arabs and Jews must meet together to achieve peace. What will you do?

- You pastor a church attended by Hollywood celebrities. A pair of movie stars asks you to perform their wedding, but you hesitate to do so. You believe both partners must have faith in God to participate in the sacred ceremony of marriage. One of these celebrities has made clear to you she has no belief in God or the Bible, but she wants a "church wedding" because it will look nice. In your mind, the sacred ceremony would be meaningless if both partners were not sincere as they participated. When you balk at performing the ceremony, the couple become indignant and threaten to tell the press how judgmental you are. Should you lower your standards to avoid bad publicity for the church?

In each of these situations, the question to ask is: "What would I do if I were not being pressured?" Clergy are expected to teach and live truth. As Dr. King said, "We are called to be people of conviction, not conformity; of moral nobility, not social respectability. We are commanded to live differently and according to a higher loyalty."

Does courage have a place in your life?

Courage is the first of human qualities because it is the quality which guarantees all others.

—Winston Churchill

Clergy can expect to encounter serious problems in their con-gregation—especially when their congregation is a prison popu-lation!

SELF-DISCIPLINE AND DILIGENCE

Like the little battery bunny, people of character just keep on going. . . .

CHAPTER SEVEN

S he has spent much of her adult life behind bars—voluntarily. She is sixty years old, though she seems much younger. She's smart, she communicates well, and she can be tough when she needs to. Her ministry demands exceptional self-discipline and diligence. She is a prison chaplain.

The women she works with have many serious problems. Ninety percent of them have drug or alcohol addictions. More than six out of ten female inmates have been victims of sexual abuse. Many of them have attempted suicide. They've been arrested, jailed, handcuffed, and searched. They've lost their friends, family, and property. Violence often intrudes into their lives. They may receive word

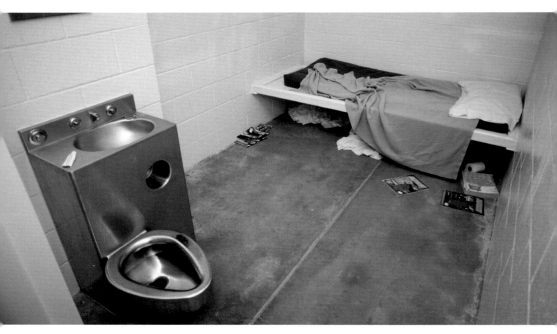

It takes self-diligence and discipline to work day after day with prison inmates.

Some Definitions

An everyday example of self-discipline is eating things that are good for you, rather than just things that taste good. Another example is controlling your behavior, even when no one is around to watch.

A trait closely related to self-discipline is diligence. Diligence is the ability to "stick with" a goal or a task until it is completed. You might have experienced a situation where the work seemed endless or so boring you thought you could never finish. But you toughed it out until completion. That is diligence. When you practice something over and over and over, or when you keep on trying something even though you are not successful at first, you show you have diligence.

in the mail that a friend died of AIDS or their husbands died in jail. They are not allowed to leave prison and attend funerals, even when a loved one dies. The chaplain says, "So mentally, socially, spiritually, in every possible way they are the most needy people you could ever meet."

She continues, "Nearly 90 percent of the women who come in here check the box that asks if they'd like to talk with me. Not just the Christians, but the Muslims, Jews and Native Americans too. I ask them how things are going. I wait, and then they start to cry. The pain is that close to the surface."

No clergy job is easy, but this one is harder than most. She has to serve inmates of every faith. She does three church services each Sunday, plus a once-a-month *sweat lodge* for Indians. She supervises the diets for Jewish and Muslim inmates. She has to see that special foods are prepared for Hanukkah and Ramadan. The majority of her work is actually spent filling out forms. The state prisons

Self-disciplined clergy make time in their lives for prayer and scripture reading.

We often think of clergy as working in safe, picturesque churches—but in reality many of them work in situations where they encounter the world's deepest problems.

want everything documented that goes on in a jail. She gets more and more inmates, but not more help to meet their needs.

She tries to spend all the time she can with the women, because it takes a long time to build up enough trust to communicate with them effectively. She spent her 60th birthday counseling an inmate with a crisis pregnancy. She listens to stories that most people would have difficulty hearing—the often brutal retelling of sexual abuse, drug use, violence, and cruelty. The women go from tough and belligerent to broken and needy. She says, "You have to have a tender heart to do this job. But you can't afford to get

In reading the lives of great men, I found that the first victory they won was over themselves ... self-discipline with all of them came first.
—Harry S. Truman

burned out. An inmate must be ready to tell you things. Even though you've heard it all before, you have to hear each person with fresh ears. You can't let it go routine."

Unlike other clergy, she has little support. The prison doesn't give her time to attend support groups or educational conferences. She says, "I don't have anybody I can talk to about my spiritual needs. This isn't a normal life. I'm not married, and I have no kids. I live on a peaceful acreage where I garden and do quiet things. My life outside is nothing like my life inside. I couldn't survive in this job if I had a husband and kids. The job is my whole life."

Clergy work requires strong characteristics of self-discipline and diligence. Self-discipline is the ability to control emotions, words, actions, and desires. It involves control, restraint, goal setting, and ability to delay gratification. Self-discipline is not easily obtained. Thomas á Kempis, a long-ago master of the spiritual life, once said: "Don't be angry that you cannot make others as you wish them to be, since you cannot make yourself as you wish to be." Hard as it is, self-discipline is necessary for anyone to be successful. King Solomon writes in the Jewish book of Proverbs, "Like a defenseless city with a broken wall is the person who lacks self-control."

> Self-discipline also means we take care of ourselves...
>
> Mahatma Gandhi, the spiritual leader of half a billion people in India, always kept every Monday as a day of silence and spiritual refreshment. Even in the midst of negotiations over India's independence from Britain, he refused to neglect this practice. He knew that without that day of rest and reflection, he would be less effective throughout the other six days of the week.

Self-discipline and diligence are vital to meet the demands placed on clergy. Dale A. Robbins, in his book *What People Ask*

Preparing a children's sermon every Sunday may be part of a pastor's job.

About the Church, writes: "In my years of traveling to hundreds of churches, I found many pastors to be some of the hardest working, most versatile, multi-skilled people I have ever met. . . . In too many cases, the pastor has to do far more than he was ever called for or even trained to do. In many churches, the pastor is often faced with having to do jobs he was never trained for—everything from plumbing to desktop publishing . . . and besides this, he also must be the well studied preacher and teacher. Beyond these demands, his life will be one of constant distractions, receiving dozens of calls and letters each day, and expected always to drop anything he's doing to sympathize, counsel, or encourage those who ask his help. The pastor seldom has enough time to do everything—time is always one of his greatest needs. . . . *There will be numerous temptations for the pastor to simply quit.*"

Women and men considering a call to serve as clergy should seriously consider whether they have the self-discipline and diligence

Sometimes the strength to "keep on keeping on" can be found in moments alone.

required. They should ask, "Am I willing to work for hours preparing meetings, when no one may show up? Am I willing to meet with people week after week for counseling, if their lives do not change for the better as a result? Am I willing to spend two days carefully preparing a sermon, and then face only negative comments? Am I willing to be on call day and night, for people who don't even show up at church on Sunday?"

Only one out of ten people who begin a clergy career will continue in ministry until the age of retirement. Steve Farrar in his book *Finishing Strong*, tells of three great young preachers—Chuck Templeton, Bron Clifford, and Billy Graham. Today, Billy Graham is obviously the most famous. Yet in 1945, the other two were more popular and successful than Billy was. At that time, people were saying Clifford would be the best preacher of the century. But nine years after that, Clifford had lost his family, his ministry, and his health. He died from complications of alcoholism at age 35. In 1950, Templeton left the ministry to pursue another career. He became discouraged with the entire Christian life. Billy Graham, however, became a household name. This was due, in part, to his possessing qualities the other two men lacked—self-discipline and diligence.

These character qualities are not only important for clergypersons. Without them, you can accomplish very little in life, no matter what your profession.

When you look at your life, do you see examples of self-discipline and diligence?

It is better to conquer yourself than to win a thousand battles. Then the victory is yours.

—Buddha

When people claim their faith as justification for their prejudice, clergy must do all they can to fight for communities that are characterized by tolerance.

CITIZENSHIP

Being a good citizen doesn't mean you're
always loyal, regardless of right and wrong.
It does mean you do what's truly best for
everyone concerned.

CHAPTER EIGHT

In the days following September 11, 2001, people around the world were fearful and angry. At a time when Americans were stricken with horror and frightened of the future, clergy from a variety of differing faiths came together in one community to build bridges for peace. Thousands of lives had been taken by an enemy few Americans realized existed. There was a new "war on terrorism." The perpetrators of the attacks were Muslims, and claimed to be acting in the name of Allah. In some communities, misguided zeal for revenge led to hate crimes against Muslims. Those whose religions required they wear a turban or a veil feared for their safety.

In Binghamton, New York, a series of rapidly formed interfaith meetings helped to educate the public and maintain calm between Muslims, Jews, and Christians. In a show of unity and peace, Imam Kasim Kopuz, the spiritual leader of the city's largest mosque, was invited to address the Friday night Sabbath service at Temple Concord on Binghamton's West Side. Imam Kopuz asked the congregation to pray for the victims of the bombing and to help relief efforts. "We will ask God to give us strength and to cure our grief," Kopuz said. "Islam requires us to take care of our neighbors. I would ask my brothers and sisters to be helpful and participate in the help effort as much as you can and pray for those who are lost."

Rabbi Michele Medwin, Temple Concord's rabbi, said "The fanatics should not be allowed to put dark masks on what religious groups really stand for. Most religious groups seek the same thing: peace and community."

People may pray and worship God in different ways—but that should not be reason for hatred or prejudice.

Citizenship means supporting our country—but some clergy believe that at times nonviolent civil disobedience may be better for the country than blind obedience.

That Sunday, the Jewish Community Center hosted another gathering organized by the Jewish Federation and the Council of Churches to discuss how the community should respond to the national tragedy. "Maybe, someday, religions of the world will have a creed of peace," said David Reaves of Endwell. Reaves, a Presbyterian, said religion cannot be used to excuse violence and hatred. "Terrorism has no religion, no prophet, and no holy book," said Imam Kopuz. U.S. Representative Maurice Hinchey, who attended Sunday's meeting, agreed. "We are not at war with Islam," said Hinchey. "If we lash out indiscriminately and kill other people, we will put ourselves in the same category as the terrorists."

The mutual cooperation of Jewish, Muslim, and Christian clergy and political leaders is an example of the character trait of citizenship. The Character Education Network defines this trait as "Being law abiding and involved in service to school, community and coun-

A Definition

Citizenship means we each do our part to make our communities better, more healthy places to live. We each have our own role to play, no matter how small. The Christian New Testament speaks of the human community as a physical body, with many parts all working together.

If the foot says, "I am not a part of the body because I am not a hand," that does not make it any less a part of the body. And if the ear says, "I am not part of the body because I am only an ear and not an eye," would that make it any less a part of the body? Suppose the whole body were an eye—then how would you hear? Or if your whole body were just one big ear, how could you smell anything? . . . What a strange thing a body would be if it had only one part! Yes, there are many parts, but only one body. The eye can never say to the hand, "I don't need you." The head can't say to the feet, "I don't need you." (1 Corinthians 12:14-17, 19-21, New Living Translation).

try." Citizenship may seem to be a simple concept. But what happens if "obeying the laws" conflicts with the demands of "service to school, community, and country?" Throughout the past several decades, some highly visible clergy have defied laws in defense of what they believe is right.

Dr. Martin Luther King, Jr. spent much of his career leading actions that broke the laws of his time. Segregation in the South was legal, and African Americans were not allowed to protest. Dr. King was committed to the idea of "nonviolent civil disobedience." That is, he deliberately broke unjust laws in ways that would harm no one. As we saw in chapter four, Father Greg's commitment to his street gang congregation sometimes has put him at odds with the police. A truly radical example of civil disobedience is Father Daniel Berrigan, the Catholic priest who has been jailed many times for trespassing at nuclear arms facilities. Convinced that nuclear weapons

Clergy can give back to their communities in many ways and many places.

would bring doom to the world unless stopped, he repeatedly went past legal boundaries to gain attention for his cause. Once he even snuck into a nuclear weapons factory and smashed up a warhead.

What do you think? Can a person be considered a good citizen if he is breaking the law? Was Dr. King justified in breaking the law so all citizens would have equal rights? Is Father Berrigan right to destroy weapons he believes will bring disaster to humanity?

As we saw earlier, there are different ways of deciding what is right. Let's examine the question, "Can someone be a good citizen and deliberately break the laws of his or her country?" We'll consider that question from Rushworth Kidder's three moral perspectives.

Ends-based thinking asks, "What is good for the greatest number of people?" In a democracy, laws usually reflect the interest of the majority of people. So ends-based thinking would frown on civil disobedience. The problem with this, though, is that minorities are bound to lose out.

Rules-based thinking asks, "What would happen if everyone followed this course of action?" Obviously, if everyone disregarded laws, the world would be rather disorderly.

As this pastor works with the children of her congregation, she is helping to build her community.

Finally, we can look at civil disobedience from the view of *care-based thinking*: "What would I want others to do for me?" Here, we see an obvious case for civil disobedience. If you were part of a minority whose rights had been denied, wouldn't you want someone to challenge the system on your behalf? If you were one of Father Greg's kids, wouldn't you want a priest to stand by your side against the police? Clergypersons tend to think of wrong and right in terms of the Golden Rule that asks that we treat others as we would like to be treated. That may explain why spiritual leaders have been the first to protest when laws are unjust.

John Carlson, a young *Lutheran* minister in Minnesota, found an unusual way to improve the system for high school seniors in his

Two groups of clergy are especially likely to be involved in public affairs outside of their congregations—rabbis and African American pastors.

Rabbis are expected to spend as much time with civic affairs as they spend caring for members of their synagogue. That's why Jewish seminaries spend much time training their graduates to be leaders in the broader community. Likewise, African American pastors often see themselves as representatives of their church in the larger public arena. Since both Jews and African Americans have suffered greatly from the insensitivity of majority groups around them, they understand the importance of having a say in local politics and service organizations.

African American pastors are especially apt to be involved with public affairs outside their congregations.

community. It didn't require him to protest anything—he just came up with a better way of doing things.

Prom night can be rough on some students. Such a big deal is made of the prom that those without dates often feel rejected. So Pastor Carlson invented the unique idea of a special party the night of the senior prom for those who did not have dates. As Tony Campolo tells the story in his book *The Kingdom of God Is a Party*, "So far as John Carlson was concerned, the prom was not the kind of party that Jesus would have liked. It was too exclusive to be Christian, in his opinion. . . . So John planned an alternative to the prom for those whom the 'system' had deemed losers and rejects. He called it the Reject Prom. Those who did not have dates were especially invited—and the kids loved it. It turned out to be a real blowout party that made the senior prom seem tame and dull by comparison."

Each year, the Reject Prom grew. Timex donated watches; then other corporations began donating prizes and gifts for the event. Eventually, even kids who did have dates began attending the Reject Prom because it was so much better than the official one.

Citizenship—improving life in our cities, schools, and nations—doesn't have to be a joyless, difficult thing. As the Reject Prom proves, it can even be fun!

In what ways do you demonstrate citizenship in your life?

You're not supposed to be so blind with patriotism that you can't face reality. Wrong is wrong, no matter who does it or who says it.

—Malcolm X

We can't save all the starfish on the beach—but we can make a difference to one!

CAREER OPPORTUNITIES

Opportunities come in many shapes and sizes . . . and some of the best have nothing to do with dollars.

CHAPTER NINE

A traveler was walking along a beach when he saw a woman scooping up starfish off the sand and tossing them into the waves. Curious, he asked her what she was doing. The woman replied, "When the tide goes out it leaves these starfish stranded on the beach. They will dry up and die before the tide comes back in, so I am throwing them back into the sea where they can live."

The traveler then said, "But this beach is miles long and there are hundreds of stranded starfish. Many will die before you reach them. Do you really think throwing back a few starfish is going to make a difference?"

The woman picked up a starfish and looked at it; then she threw it into the waves. "It makes a difference to this one," she said.

As our culture changes, more and more churches are empty.

This story, attributed to Loren Eisely, could serve as an illustration of the way many clergy view success in their careers. In other vocations, hard work is expected to bring more power, bigger pay, and more prestige. That rarely happens in ministry. Spiritual leaders must see success defined in terms of individuals whose lives have been transformed rather than material rewards.

Shrinking Churches

In 2011, the average Protestant church shrunk. Methodist churches declined 1.01 percent, American Baptist churches declined 1.55 percent, and Presbyterian churches declined 2.61 percent, among others.

In some cases, ministers and rabbis who show exceptional talent will be called to serve in bigger churches or synagogues. It is also possible that their congregations will grow larger, and thus be able to pay larger salaries. Realistically, however, both Christian and Jewish congregations are diminishing in size throughout North America. With churches, monasteries, and synagogues shrinking, it is obvious that few clergy will have the opportunity to go to larger congregations or expect sizable increases in pay.

Their relatively low salaries reflect a traditional understanding that ministers do not choose their vocation for the sake of money. The very word, "clergy" reflects this. The root is the Greek word *kleros*, which means "inheritance." Early Christian priests were called by that word to remind people of Deuteronomy 18:2: "Therefore [the priests] shall have no inheritance among their brothers and sisters: the Lord is their inheritance." That was understood as God's way of saying, "I'll provide for the priests, but they shouldn't expect to be paid much."

The opportunities for clergypersons depend on the religious group. For instance, the Roman Catholic church in North America faces a severe shortage of priests. Catholic immigrants have actually increased the overall attendance of American Catholic churches. At the same time, the number of young men entering seminaries is far

Opportunities for clergy vary from church to church.

too few to meet the number of positions open in the churches. Meanwhile, job openings for Protestant ministers vary greatly, depending on the type of church. In the so-called "mainstream" churches (Episcopal, Methodist, Presbyterian, and Congregational), the majority of ministers are nearing retirement age. Small rural churches in those denominations have in some cases hired untrained and unlicensed people to serve as pastors to keep the churches from closing down. Job prospects are good for seminary-trained graduates in these denominational churches.

Open positions are much scarcer in Evangelical churches. There are many seminary graduates seeking churches, and relatively few openings. Prospects are good for pastors willing to work

Judaism is thriving in North America, and opportunities for rabbis are excellent.

Today, Orthodox rabbis are always male, but in Reformed and Conservative Jewish synagogues there are growing numbers of women rabbis.

in poor rural churches, but large city churches are very hard to get. An Evangelical church looking for a pastor is likely to get 400 applications, from which one pastor will be selected.

Job opportunities for rabbis are excellent in all four of the major branches of Judaism. There are many synagogues seeking rabbis, and many have rabbis who are near retirement.

Gender and marriage status are important factors in clergy career choices. Orthodox Judaism, Greek Orthodoxy, Roman Catholicism, Christian fundamentalism, and all branches of Islam refuse to accept women as spiritual leaders. Women can serve as pastors in mainstream Protestant denominations, though they are less likely than men to pastor large urban churches. Women can serve as rabbis in Reformed and Conservative Jewish synagogues. A former president of the Conservative Jewish Movement in America was a

Not Exactly Big Bucks

The pay for Roman Catholic priests averaged $12,936 per year in 1998. Salary, however, is only part of the way priests are compensated. The church usually provides car allowance, room and board in the parish rectory, health insurance, and a retirement plan. The value of all these benefits combined in 1998 came to around $30,000. Salaries of Protestant clergy vary substantially, depending on experience, denomination, size, and wealth of the congregation, and geographic location. Clergy in different religions tend to make different amounts of money. In 2012, rabbis earned the most money on average—$140,000, including housing. Christian clergy tended to make less, although leaders of megachurches (churches with more than 2,000 people) earn just as much. Protestant clergy at smaller churches made an average of $40,000, while Roman Catholic priests make even less at $25,000 a year. Imams in mosques make around $30,000 a year, and do not usually get money for housing like some other clergy.

woman, Judy Yudof. Evangelical churches vary in their acceptance of female leadership. Some believe the Bible requires senior pastors to be male. Other Evangelicals believe Scripture has been misinterpreted to exclude women. A woman seeking to serve as pastor in Evangelical churches must approach congregations on a case-by-case basis to learn if they are open to a female leader.

Marriage is also an issue that must be considered for careers in ministry. The Roman Catholic church will only allow unmarried priests. This is a major reason for the shortage of priests in North America today; celibacy is not a popular option for most young men. Protestant churches represent the opposite extreme; while no group has actual rules requiring pastors to be married, there is a very strong bias toward hiring married pastors.

Clergy work harder for less pay than other professionals with the same amount of training. They are unlikely to gain greater financial compensation, greater prestige, or greater opportunities as they work through their careers. They are held to the very highest standards of character. They work longer hours than people in comparable professions like counseling and social services. There are many challenges and discouragements. So why would anyone want to be a clergyperson?

As mentioned in Chapter 1, spiritual leaders feel God has

True Wealth

When a traveler at last comes home from a far journey, with what gladness his family and his friends receive him! Even so shall your good deeds welcome you like friends and with what rejoicing when you pass from this life to the next!

—Buddha

Clergy provide guidance at life's happiest and most crucial moments.

chosen them to serve him. This sense of being "called" sets the ministry apart from ordinary career choices. Faith in God's call enables clergy to remain optimistic despite circumstances. Studies have determined what factors enable clergy to succeed against the odds in their profession. Clergypersons who are most likely to succeed are those who have a strong personal conviction that God has chosen them for this career.

Many careers offer good pay and good benefits, but very little sense of having improved people's lives. For spiritual leaders, it is just the opposite. Clergy should expect little tangible reward—yet they are constantly given opportunities to benefit others. They provide guidance at life's most crucial intersections: birth, marriage, and death. They are given access to the innermost depths of men's and women's souls. They create services that place renewed confidence in struggling lives. When there appears to be no hope on earth, clergy point to a deeper, more lasting hope.

Despite the daunting challenges, clergy experience nonmaterial benefits that truly outweigh the difficulties they face. For Bennie Newton, it was seeing an alcoholic dry up and begin a sober life. For Sister Nancy, it is seeing a homeless woman gain employment and leave the street. For Father Greg, it is seeing one of his homeboys forswear violence. Dr. Martin Luther King, Jr. rejoiced seeing that African Americans were nearing the promised land of equal opportunity. A prison chaplain creates a sense of hope for inmates who must spend their lives behind bars. The choices each of these clergypersons made have changed the world in real and permanent ways.

After reading this book, you may or may not want to consider a future as a member of the clergy. Either way, however, you can choose to live out the core qualities of good character. When you do, you too will experience the power to make our world a better place.

The abundance of life does not consist of material possessions.
                                                        —Jesus

Further Reading

Fremon, Celeste. *G-Dog and the Homeboys: Father Greg Boyle and the Gangs of East Los Angeles*. Albuquerque, New Mex.: University of New Mexico Press, 2008.

Kaylin, Lucy. *For the Love of God: The Faith and Future of the American Nun*. New York: Harper Perennial, 2001.

Kidder, Rushworth M. *How Good People Make Tough Choices*. New York: HarperCollins, 2009.

Carson, Clayborne. *The Autobiography of Martin Luther King, Jr.* Boston, Mass.: Grand Central Publishing, 2001.

Ulfstein, Stefan. *Pastors Off the Record*. Downers Grove, Ill.: Intervarsity Press, 1993.

Wilkes, Paul. *And They Shall Be My People: An American Rabbi and His Congregation*. New York: Grove Press, 2000.

For More Information

Barna Research Online
(up-to-date information on religion in America)
www.barna.org

Center for the 4th and 5th Rs
www.cortland.edu/c4n5rs

Character Education Network
www.charactered.net

College Graduate Career Information
(up-to-date information on clergy and other careers: education, salary, job prospects, duties, and useful tips)
www.collegegrad.com

The Josephson Institute of Ethics
(information on character traits, ethics and decision making)
www.josephsoninstitute.org

Publisher's Note:
The websites on this page were active at the time of publication. The publisher is not responsible for websites that have changed their address or discontinued operation since the date of publication. The publisher will review and update the websites upon each reprint.

Glossary

Barrio   A Mexican neighborhood.

Bible college   A special Protestant college where students focus on studying the Bible.

Big Apple   A nickname for New York City.

Jesuit   A Catholic order of monks, founded by Ignatius Loyola in the 16th century, devoted to education and missionary work.

Laypersons   People in a church who are not clergy.

Lutheran   One of the mainline Protestant denominations, begun by Martin Luther in the 16th century.

Parish   A section of the population that attends one church.

Pimping   Selling a woman as a prostitute.

Presbyterian   One of the mainline Protestant denominations, it has a hierarchy of officials that govern the church.

Protestant   Any Christian who is not Catholic or Greek Orthodox.

Seminary   A college for training people to be clergy.

Sweat lodge   A hut or cave heated by steam from water poured on hot stones, used in Native American spiritual rituals.

Index

About the Author & Consultants

Kenneth McIntosh taught in a Los Angeles middle school for nine years, then felt called to the ministry. He attended Fuller Seminary while preaching at a small church in Southern California. He is currently the minister at a church in Flagstaff, Arizona.

Ernestine G. Riggs is an associate professor at Loyola University Chicago. She has been involved in the field of education for more than forty years and has a diverse background in teaching and administration. Riggs was selected as one of the Outstanding Elementary Teachers of America by the United States Department of Defense Overseas Schools in 1974. She is the coauthor of *Beyond Rhetoric and Rainbows: A Journey to the Place Where Learning Lives*, *Helping Middle and High School Readers: Teaching and Learning Strategies Across the Curriculum*, and several journal articles. She is also co-featured in the video *Ensuring Success for "Low Yield" Students: Building Lives and Molding Futures*. In the summer of 2007, Riggs was invited to present a précis of the research on conation at the prestigious Oxford Round Table in Oxford, England. Riggs is a frequent presenter at local, district, national, and international conferences.

Cheryl R. Gholar has been a teacher, counselor, and administrator in public schools and worked in postsecondary education for more than thirty years. She is associate director of the Professional Development Consortium. Gholar is coauthor of *Beyond Rhetoric and Rainbows: A Journey to the Place Where Learning Lives*. She is also co-featured in the video *Ensuring Success for "Low Yield" Students: Building Lives and Molding Futures*. She is published in *Vitae Scholasticae*, *Black Issues in Higher Education*, *The Journal of Staff Development*, *Careers With Character*, and more. Gholar's awards include Educator of the Year; Phi Delta Kappa; Those Who Excel; Oppenheimer Family Foundation; Outstanding Teacher, Chicago Region PTA; and Outstanding Contributions to The Department of Character Education, Chicago Public Schools.